FROM SEA to SHINING SEA

WYOMING

ALEXANDRA HANSON-HARDING

Consultants

MELISSA N. MATUSEVICH, PH.D.

Curriculum and Instruction Specialist
Blacksburg, Virginia

TRACEY KINNAMAN

Children's Librarian
Hot Springs County Library
Thermopolis, Wyoming

VALERIE ROADY

District Library Media Specialist
Big Horn County School District #4
Basin, Wyoming

CHILDREN'S PRESS®

A DIVISION OF SCHOLASTIC INC.

New York • Toronto • London • Auckland • Sydney • Mexico City
New Delhi • Hong Kong • Danbury, Connecticut

Wyoming is a Rocky Mountain state. It is bordered by Montana, South Dakota, Nebraska, Colorado, Utah, and Idaho.

The photograph on the front cover shows whitewater rafters on the Shoshone River.

Project Editor: Meredith DeSousa
Art Director: Marie O'Neill
Photo Researcher: Marybeth Kavanagh
Design: Robin West, Ox and Company, Inc.
Page 6 map and recipe art: Susan Hunt Yule
All other maps: XNR Productions, Inc.

Library of Congress Cataloging-in-Publication Data

Hanson-Harding, Alexandra.
      Wyoming / Alexandra Hanson-Harding.
         p. cm. – (From sea to shining sea)
      Summary: An introduction to the state of Wyoming, describing its geography, history,
government, people, economy, and more. Includes bibliographical references and index.
   ISBN 0-516-22490-5
      1. Wyoming—Juvenile literature. [1. Wyoming.] I. Title. II. Series.

F761.3 .H36 2003
978.7—dc21   2002014294

TABLE of CONTENTS

CHAPTER ONE

INTRODUCING THE EQUALITY STATE

Wyoming is a Rocky Mountain state that offers backcountry adventures and western hospitality.

Wyoming is a land of wide-open spaces. It has wild, windswept plains and majestic mountains. It has deserts with shifting sands, and deep-green forests of aspen, fir, and ponderosa pine. These lands are rich with animal life, including pronghorn antelopes, buffalos, elk, grizzly bears, wolves, and coyotes.

Wyoming is also home to almost 500,000 people, many of whom work, live, and play in its busy cities and towns. Across the state, workers operate oil rigs, and farmers manage vast sugar-beet farms. Miners extract uranium ore from Wyoming's mineral-rich land.

Throughout history, Wyoming has been known for its hardy pioneers, hard-working cowboys, and tough cattle and sheep ranchers. In many ways, Wyoming was far ahead of its time. Women in Wyoming won the right to vote in 1869, before any other state in the union. They were also the first to serve on juries and to hold public office. These courageous "firsts" on behalf of women earned Wyoming the nickname the Equality State.

What else comes to mind when you think of Wyoming?

- ❖ Arapaho Indians hunting buffalo on the plains
- ❖ Skiers whooshing down mountain slopes
- ❖ Scientists unearthing ancient dinosaur bones from fossil beds
- ❖ Boiling-hot water spouting from the famous geyser Old Faithful
- ❖ Vast fields of bubbling volcanic mud in Yellowstone National Park
- ❖ The spicy scent of sagebrush blowing on the wind
- ❖ The gigantic Grand Teton Mountains towering above vast plains
- ❖ Devil's Tower, the nation's first national monument; Yellowstone, the nation's first national park; and Shoshone, the nation's first national forest
- ❖ Cowboys roping steers during Frontier Days
- ❖ Oil wells on the open prairie

The harsh but powerful land of Wyoming is a place where rugged individualists have thrived. It is a place full of history and beauty. It is a place where you can find wild animals and a landscape that has inspired writers and artists. Turn the page to learn about the exciting adventure that is Wyoming.

Gillette

Casper

Rock Springs

Laramie

Cheyenne

CHEYENNE FRONTIER DAYS

©SHY03

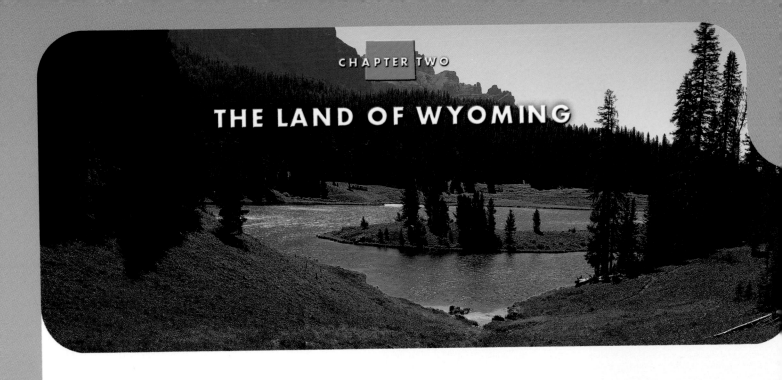

CHAPTER TWO

THE LAND OF WYOMING

Anyone with a ruler could easily draw a map of Wyoming—it is the shape of a rectangle. Wyoming is located in the Rocky Mountain region of the United States, an area that divides the Midwest from the West. Surrounding Wyoming is Montana to the north, South Dakota and Nebraska to the east, Colorado and Utah to the south, and Utah and Idaho to the west.

Wyoming is the ninth largest state in total area. You could fit all of the New England states (Maine, Vermont, New Hampshire, Massachusetts, Rhode Island, and Connecticut) plus Delaware, New Jersey, Maryland, and the island of Hawaii inside of Wyoming's 97,914 square miles (253,597 square kilometers).

Wyoming is also the second highest state in the country, with an average elevation (height above sea level) of 6,700 feet (2,042 meters). Only Colorado's average elevation of 6,800 feet (2,073 m) is higher.

Shoshone National Forest has rolling meadows, rugged mountains, and clear lakes.

The state's lowest elevation is in the Great Plains at the Belle Fourche River. The land there is 3,099 feet (945 m) above sea level.

Most of Wyoming is higher than one mile (1.6 kilometers) above sea level.

Four distinct geographical regions make up the state. They are the Great Plains, the mountains, the intermontane basins, and the Yellowstone area.

GREAT PLAINS

About one-third of Wyoming's land—the east and northeast portions—lie within the Great Plains. It is a huge area of relatively high, flat land that starts in Texas and stretches all the way up to northern Canada. This region is about 300 to 700 miles (483 to 1,127 km) wide, and its western boundary is the Rocky Mountains.

The western part of the Great Plains, where Wyoming is located, is semiarid (dry). There are few trees, except by the banks of rivers, in the foothills of the Rocky Mountains, and in the Black Hills region, which borders South Dakota on the east. Instead, tough native grasses cover most of the region.

Although it is a dry area, some parts of Wyoming's plains have been turned into productive farmland. In recent times, farmers have found ways to irrigate (bring in a regular supply of water from lakes and rivers), which allows them to water crops. However, the plains are used mostly as rangeland for cattle and sheep.

MOUNTAINS

Wyoming is part of the Continental Divide, a line across the continent that divides waters flowing east from those flowing west. In the United States, the Continental Divide closely follows the top, or crest line, of the Rocky Mountains from Canada to Mexico, crossing through the states of Montana, Wyoming, Colorado, and New Mexico. The Rockies do not trace a neat line north to south, however; they are broken into many smaller chains.

The Rockies enter Wyoming in the northwest corner, near Yellowstone National Park. In that region are the Absaroka, Teton, Gros

The Teton Range appears to rise straight up from the plains.

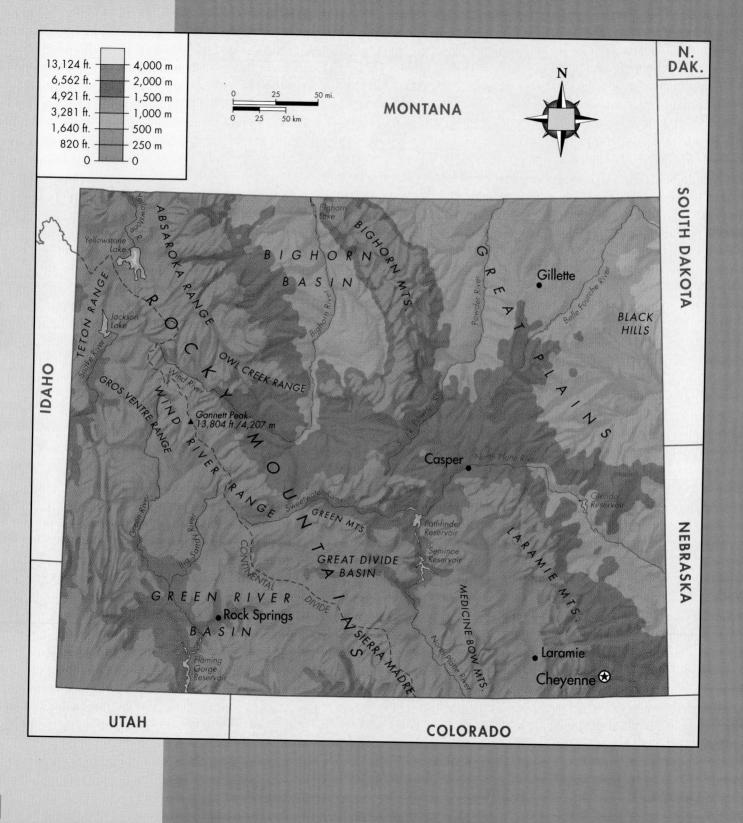

MONTANA

N

13,124 ft.	4,000 m
6,562 ft.	2,000 m
4,921 ft.	1,500 m
3,281 ft.	1,000 m
1,640 ft.	500 m
820 ft.	250 m
0	0

0   25   50 mi.

0   25   50 km

N. DAK.

SOUTH DAKOTA

NEBRASKA

UTAH

COLORADO

IDAHO

Yellowstone Lake

Yellowstone R.

ABSAROKA RANGE

TETON RANGE

Jackson Lake

Snake River

GROS VENTRE RANGE

ROCKY

WIND RIVER RANGE

Wind River

OWL CREEK RANGE

BIGHORN BASIN

Bighorn Lake

BIGHORN MTS.

Bighorn River

GREAT

Powder River

PLAINS

Gillette

Belle Fourche River

BLACK HILLS

▲ Gannett Peak
13,804 ft./4,207 m

MOUNTAINS

Green River

Big Sandy River

Sweetwater River

GREEN MTS.

CONTINENTAL DIVIDE

GREAT DIVIDE BASIN

Ft. Powder R.

Casper

North Platte River

Pathfinder Reservoir

Seminoe Reservoir

Glendo Reservoir

LARAMIE MTS.

GREEN RIVER BASIN

Rock Springs

SIERRA MADRE

MEDICINE BOW MTS.

North Platte River

Laramie

Cheyenne ✪

Flaming Gorge Reservoir

Ventre, Wind River, and Owl Creek ranges. The state's highest point of elevation, Gannett Peak, belongs to part of the Wind River Range.

Mountain ranges in southeastern Wyoming are the Laramie, Medicine Bow, and Sierra Madre. The western edge of the lower-lying Black Hills is in northeastern Wyoming. They are only about 6,000 feet (1,829 m) high on average. They are called the Black Hills because they are covered with ponderosa pines, which look dark—almost black— from a distance.

INTERMONTANE BASINS

Trapped between the mighty mountain ranges are several intermontane basins. *Intermontane* means "between mountains." A basin is a wide valley ringed by hills or mountains. There are three major basins in Wyoming. The Bighorn Basin lies in northwestern Wyoming. South of the Owl Creek Mountains lies the smaller Shoshone Basin. Farther south is the largest basin, the Great Divide Basin.

The Great Divide Basin is at a very high elevation. Water that falls there stays in the basin and does not flow to the Atlantic or Pacific Ocean. But the basin is so dry that water almost always evaporates (changes into vapor) before hitting the ground. Part of the Great Divide Basin is made up of the Red Desert, one of the largest cold deserts in the United States. Cold deserts get most of the little water they receive in the form of snow. The Red Desert is so dry that one section, the

The Killpecker sand dunes constantly shift as the wind blows.

Killpecker Dune Field, is full of huge sand dunes. Some of these sand dunes are 150 feet (46 m) high!

Many creatures call the Great Divide Basin home. Desert herds of wild elk thunder past rainbow-colored cliffs. Hawks circle overhead looking for prairie dogs. Bobcats and mountain lions hunt for prey near extinct volcanoes. Sheep graze there, as well.

FIND OUT MORE

The Great Divide Basin is home to about five thousand wild horses—one of the largest wild-horse herds in the United States. How might herds of wild horses have developed in this region?

YELLOWSTONE

Can you imagine a place where water suddenly spurts into the sky, where mud bubbles out of the earth, and where mineral deposits make pools of water look cornflower-blue? There is such a place in Wyoming—it is Yellowstone National Park.

At 3,472 square miles (8,992 sq km), Yellowstone is larger than the state of Delaware. Most of Yellowstone is inside Wyoming's borders, though small portions of it are in Montana and Idaho.

Yellowstone is home to more than 200 geysers. Geysers are hot springs that can shoot steam and water hundreds of feet into the air. They are found in areas with lots of volcanic activity. Rainwater that seeps into the earth near geysers moves through long tunnels deep below the earth's surface. The water is heated by the hot melted rock deep underground. When the water gets hot enough, it spurts into the air. One of the most well-known geysers is Old Faithful, which erupts on a regular schedule.

Yellowstone has many other natural wonders, such as beautiful Yellowstone Canyon. Yellowstone

Old Faithful erupts every 61 to 67 minutes. A single eruption lasts 2 to 5 minutes.

Canyon was formed thousands of years ago, as water cut through layers of volcanic rock. The Yellowstone River moves through this canyon, which is made of a soft yellow rock called rhyolite. Over time, water has worn away the rock in the river's path. The river rushes over Yellowstone Falls, which is divided into the upper and the lower falls. The lower falls is the highest in the park, at 308 feet (94 m).

People come from all over the world to see the incredible wildlife at Yellowstone, including elk, trumpeter swans, bison, and wolves. Many black bears and grizzly bears also live in the park. At one time, about 50,000 grizzly bears lived in the West. Now, only about 1,000 grizzlies live south of Canada. The largest concentration of grizzlies lives in and around Yellowstone National Park.

EXTRA! EXTRA!

For many years, Yellowstone's grizzlies were famous for raiding campsites, eating hot dogs, hamburgers, and other leftovers. They also feasted at garbage dumps. Because these powerful animals can be dangerous to humans, the National Park Service closed the dumps in an effort to force bears to find berries, fish, and other natural foods. Many bears were even killed. In recent years, the bear population in Yellowstone has been increasing, but more efforts are needed to reduce conflicts between bears and people.

WATER

All rivers east of the Continental Divide flow into the Missouri River Basin and eventually into the Atlantic Ocean. The 682-mile-

(1,098-km-) long Yellowstone River begins in Yellowstone National Park and heads northeast until it meets the Missouri River at the border of North Dakota. Other Wyoming rivers whose waters find their way to the Atlantic include the Platte, Belle Fourche, Wind, and Bighorn. The Platte River is very important because it provides water for several reservoirs and is a major source of drinking water.

The rivers west of the divide flow into the Columbia or Colorado River Basin and eventually into the Pacific Ocean. The source of the Snake River is in western Wyoming, where people enjoy rafting in its fast-moving waters. The Green River drains into the Colorado River, which flows into the Gulf of California in Mexico.

There are also a number of reservoirs in the state. The Green River is dammed 15 miles (24 km) south of Wyoming in Utah. The dam blocked the flow of water and created the Flaming Gorge Reservoir, part of the Flaming Gorge National Recreation Area. People can boat, camp, and enjoy the scenery at this huge reservoir. Other major reservoirs include the Pathfinder, Glendo, and Seminoe reservoirs, part of which come from the waters of the North Platte River. Fontanelle Reservoir was also formed by a dam on the Green River.

The Snake River winds its way through some of the most beautiful scenery in the United States.

Yellowstone Lake is Wyoming's largest and deepest natural lake. It covers an area of 136 square miles (352 sq km). In some areas it is 300 feet (91 m) deep. Jackson Lake, the second largest in Wyoming, covers 40 square miles (104 sq km). Some of Wyoming's other lakes include the DeSmet and Shoshone lakes. Bighorn Lake, an artificial lake near the Bighorn Canyon National Recreation Area, comes from the waters of the Green River.

Energy produced by these wind turbines provides enough electricity for 27,000 homes.

CLIMATE

The weather in Wyoming is generally cool, dry, and windy. High land and mountain ridges trap and funnel air to create wind. The average wind speed is nearly 13 miles per hour (21 kilometers per hour). Casper, Wyoming, is the fifth windiest city in the nation. In fact, Wyoming is one of the leading states for harvesting wind power for energy.

Overall, it does not rain much in Wyoming. The average yearly rainfall is 14.5 inches (37 centimeters), but rainfall can vary greatly across the state. The mountains affect Wyoming's weather. Weather generally moves west to east. Tall mountains can trap rainfall, leaving the eastern areas dry. Some places high in the mountains have snow year-round. Because the climate varies around the state, some areas get as little as 5 inches (13 cm) of rain or snow per year, while others may get up to 45 inches (114 cm) annually.

Wyoming's weather can change suddenly. In August 2000, Wyoming was so dry that forest fires burned thousands of acres in Devils Tower National Park. Drought also dried up wells throughout the state. Less than a month later, a severe blizzard stranded hundreds of Wyoming motorists across the state. Blizzards do not occur every winter in Wyoming, but they are always a danger.

Because of its high altitude, Wyoming has the second coolest climate of the continental United States. The state's normal mean temperature is 45.6° Fahrenheit (8° Celsius). The average winter temperature is 19° F (–7° C). The lowest temperature ever recorded in Wyoming was –66° F (–54° C), recorded on February 9, 1933 at Moran, near Elk.

Wyoming residents enjoy the winter weather at the Jackson Hole cutter races.

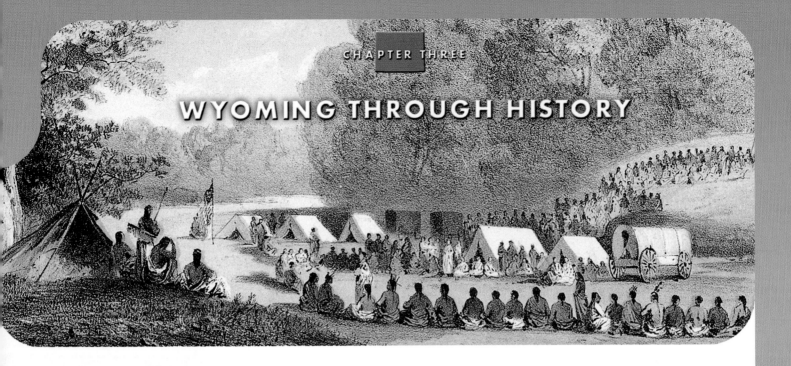

CHAPTER THREE

WYOMING THROUGH HISTORY

The Gros Ventre were one of the earliest Native American groups to live in Wyoming.

For thousands of years Native Americans have made their home in Wyoming's vast plains, valleys, and mountains. Some of the earliest people who lived in what is now Wyoming include the Clovis (12,000 years ago) and the Folsom (10,000 years ago). Scientists call these people Paleo-Indians (*paleo* is a Greek word meaning "old"). Paleo-Indians lived in Wyoming (and across much of the West) at the end of the Ice Age, when life was very different than it is today.

They survived by gathering plants and hunting animals such as woolly mammoths, a kind of hairy elephant that is now extinct. The Clovis and the Folsom also hunted creatures such as bison (buffalo) and elk. Modern scientists have found special arrowheads that the Clovis and the Folsom once used to hunt these animals. Eventually, because the climate changed and because of overhunting, many of these creatures died out, or became extinct.

Around 7000 B.C., Wyoming became drier, and many of the animals that people relied on for food and clothing moved away in search of grassier fields and more water. Most of the humans followed the animals, and left Wyoming. People started to come back around 4500 B.C. but in small numbers. It was still difficult to survive on this land. There were many bison, but they were hard to hunt on foot. Also, the dry land made it difficult to farm or gather food.

Things changed in the early 1700s. Wyoming's plains became home to Native American groups who developed a distinctive lifestyle we now associate with the Plains Indians. These peoples survived by hunting the vast herds of buffalo, but they had something to help them—horses. In the early 1600s the Spanish began to set up missions in the Southwest and brought horses with them. Native American groups in the Southwest traded for horses, impressed by these powerful, useful animals. Other horses escaped and were captured by Native Americans. Soon, Native American peoples all over the West were using horses for traveling, hunting, and warfare. Horses were especially useful for hunting the fast-moving herds of bison that lived on the plains. By the 1750s, members of most Plains Indian tribes had acquired horses.

Plains Indians eventually grew skilled at riding horses. This illustration shows Native Americans horse-racing.

Buffalo were important to these tribes. The main people who inhabited Wyoming's plains, including the Shoshone and the Cheyenne, lived in painted buffalo-skin tents. They used the meat of the buffalo for food and the skin for clothing and blankets. They even sewed their clothes with needles made of buffalo bone. As one elderly Kiowa woman said, "The buffalo were the life of the Kiowa."

A number of different peoples lived in the area. They included the Cheyenne, who lived mostly in eastern Wyoming; the Crow, who lived in the Powder, Big Horn, and Wind River valleys in the central and western parts of the state; and the Gros Ventre, the Kiowa, the Nez Perce, the Sheep Eater, and the Sioux, who also lived in eastern Wyoming. Other tribes in the area were the Pawnee, the Shoshone, and the Ute, among others. These groups sometimes fought with one another. The Cheyenne and the Sioux, for example, had so much military power that they were able to force weaker groups out of the best bison-hunting lands onto less-inhabited lands in Wyoming.

FIND OUT MORE

The Medicine Wheel is a mysterious circle of stones located on Medicine Mountain in north central Wyoming. It is 245 feet (75 m) around and has 28 spokes. No one knows who created it or why. A Crow Indian chief once said, "It was built before the light came, by people who had no iron." Some believe that the Medicine Wheel had some kind of religious or spiritual importance to its creators. For what reasons do you think an ancient people might have built it?

EXPLORATION AND FUR-TRADING DAYS

At the turn of the century, United States President Thomas Jefferson became eager to explore the unchartered West. In 1804 he sent an expedition, led by Meriwether Lewis and William Clark, to learn about and map the area. Although the group bypassed Wyoming on their journey west, one member, John Colter, left to explore on his own. In 1807, he became the first white man to explore Wyoming's Yellowstone area.

Yellowstone's geysers, hot springs, and other natural wonders amazed Colter. Because of his reports of how the earth steamed and boiled there, the area was nicknamed Colter's Hell. Later, this place became known as Yellowstone, after the Native American name for the Yellowstone River, *Mi tsi a da zi,* which means "rock yellow river." The yellow color comes from the yellow rhyolite stone found in the area.

Many of the earliest explorers in Wyoming were fur trappers who came to the region to find beaver pelts. In 1811, an explorer named Wilson Price Hunt crossed Wyoming. He was sent by John Jacob

Mammoth Springs was one of Wyoming's most unusual land features.

Astor, a rich New York businessman and founder of the American Fur Company. Astor wanted Hunt to find places to gather beaver furs. The furs would then be made into fashionable hats and sold in stores. Hunt led an expedition from St. Louis, Missouri, to the Pacific Coast, exploring Wyoming on the way. He crossed the Great Plains, the Bighorn Mountains, the Wind River, and the Green River and later reported his findings.

Native Americans were skilled fur trappers.

The next year, explorer Robert Stuart's party found a pass in the tall, rugged chain of the Rocky Mountains. (A pass is a low place between two mountain peaks.) The route they took would later become part of the Oregon Trail, a route that was commonly used by settlers to travel west.

Over time, more fur trappers came to Wyoming. These "mountain men" took their furs to trading posts and traded the furs for money. Every year, the trappers met and exchanged information about the land. Together, they mapped out much of this rugged territory. One of the most famous mountain men to make a home in Wyoming was James Beckwourth. He was an African-American from Missouri who fled slavery. He became a fur trapper and worked with the Rocky Mountain Fur Company. Later he was welcomed into a Crow Indian family, with whom he lived for several years. Afterward, Beckwourth was a guide and messenger, helping to lead travelers across the rugged mountains and delivering messages from one place to another. He discovered the famous Beckwourth Pass and later set up a trading post.

James Beckwourth discovered a pass through the Sierra Nevada Mountains.

Nearly half a million people went west on the Oregon Trail.

HEADING WEST ON THE OREGON TRAIL

In 1834, Fort Laramie was built in southeast Wyoming, at present-day Laramie. It was Wyoming's first permanent trading post. By that time, interest in trapping was beginning to wane. Trappers had depleted most of the beavers, and eventually beaver hats went out of style.

In the early 1840s, many fur trappers began to do a new kind of work. During this time, people from the eastern United States and Europe felt crowded and wanted open land. They had heard that the Oregon Territory had rich, fertile land for farming.

Pioneers in covered wagons began to push through Wyoming on their way to the Oregon Territory. The fur traders helped people who were traveling west, leading groups, giving them advice, and selling them needed goods at trading posts. Pioneers faced a difficult journey. They crossed mountains and rode through dusty deserts. Traveling at a rate of just 15 miles (24 km) per day, they had to complete the entire 2,000-mile (3,219-km) journey in about five months—or else they would face getting trapped by snow.

Many people died of cholera and other diseases, such as the tick-born "mountain fever," along the way. Sometimes people were left to die alone by the side of a road. There were other dangers as well. Mary Ackley, a young pioneer girl, wrote about crossing the swift Green River. "One man started to ford the river in a wagon with two of his children," she wrote. "The wagon body floated off and went a mile downstream before it was rescued. One daughter, who was twelve years old, saved herself and the life of her little sister, two years old, by catching hold of the wagon bows and holding her little sister's head above the water." It is estimated that of the 300,000 to 500,000 people who

Most settlers used oxen to pull their wagons. Oxen were strong but slow, traveling only 2 miles (3 km) per hour.

went west between 1840 and 1870, about 20,000 to 30,000 people died on the trail.

STRUGGLES WITH NATIVE AMERICANS

Over time, Native Americans began to grow angry as more and more pioneers pushed west. They looked upon the pioneers as trespassers and feared that they would steal their land, as white people had done to Native Americans in the East. In addition, thousands of Native Americans were killed by diseases the pioneers brought west. Other Native Americans went hungry, as white settlers killed vast numbers of buffalo.

United States Army soldiers established forts along the route to protect travelers from the Native Americans, who sometimes attacked wagon trains. In 1851 some Native American tribes met with United States government agents at Fort Laramie to sign a formal agreement called a treaty. For $50,000 per year, Native Americans would allow pioneers to travel through their land—but not settle on it. The United States did not keep this commitment, and soon broke the treaty.

Trouble erupted with the Sioux in 1854 and then with the Cheyenne in 1857. Conflicts continued throughout the 1860s, as more Americans began to settle in Wyoming. To make things worse, the United States government claimed even more land to build a railroad. Then, after gold was discovered in Bozeman and Virginia City in Montana, the government

Red Cloud was one of the most important leaders of the Lakota.

wanted to build a trail to the gold fields through one of the Sioux's most plentiful hunting grounds. Soon, the Oglala Sioux Indians were pushed from their homeland onto a smaller area north of the Platte River. Their leader, Red Cloud, said, "When the white man comes in my country, he leaves a trail of blood behind him . . . I have two mountains in that country—the Black Hills and the Big Horn Mountain. I want the Great Father to make no roads through them."

Although Red Cloud refused to sign a treaty, the United States government built three forts along the trail. One was Fort Phil Kearney. Members of the United States Cavalry who were stationed there fought many battles with thousands of skilled Native American fighters from the Arapaho, Cheyenne, and Sioux tribes. An unknown number of Native Americans died in these battles. The year 1865 was called the Bloody Year of the Plains because the fighting was so intense.

Not all Native Americans were hostile to the settlers. Chief Washakie of the Shoshone decided that it was useless to fight these powerful settlers from the East. He was an ally to white pioneers. He helped the United States Army fight against hostile tribes and allowed white travelers to pass through Shoshone land. Later he was given a reservation, or piece of land for his people to share, in Wyoming's Wind River Valley.

FIND OUT MORE

The struggle between settlers and Native Americans was not the only important historical event of the 1860s. What other major event took place during that decade?

Other Native Americans struggled to maintain control of their lands. But eventually they were overcome by the military power of the United States. "The white people have surrounded me," Chief Red Cloud said, "and left me nothing but an island. When we first had this land, we were strong. Now we are melting like snow on the hillside, while you are growing like spring grass . . ." By the late 1870s, most Native Americans, including Red Cloud and his people, were forced onto reservations.

Today the Wind River Reservation is home to the Eastern Shoshone and Northern Arapaho tribes. It is the third largest Native American reservation in the country.

In 1866 the Laramie County Public Library System was organized. It was the first county public library system in the U.S.

Wapiti Ranger Station was established in the Shoshone National Forest in 1891. It was the first U.S. ranger station.

Mrs. Estelle Reel was elected superintendent of public instruction in 1894. She became the first woman to be elected to a statewide position.

LINKING EAST AND WEST

In 1860 a new kind of mail service, called the Pony Express, was born. It promised to bring mail from east to west in a lightning-fast ten days. Pony Express riders traveled between Sacramento, California, and St. Joseph, Missouri, passing through Wyoming. The riders risked their lives, covering more than 650,000 miles (1,046,074 km) to deliver 34,753 pieces of mail. They lost only one mailbag over the lifetime of the Pony Express. A year and a half later, telegraph service linked the West to the rest of the United States, allowing messages to be sent instantaneously across the country. (A telegraph is a device for sending messages over a wire by using a code of electrical signals.) The Pony Express was out of business.

During the 1860s, the land that was to be Wyoming became part of one of the most exciting advances in transportation in United States history. In 1862, President Abraham Lincoln signed the Pacific Railroad Act. Under this act, the Central Pacific Railroad began laying railroad tracks eastward from California. At the same time, the Union Pacific began building west from Omaha, Nebraska, passing through Wyoming. They would lay 1,700 miles (2,736 km) of track between them.

This illustration shows Sherman Station in Wyoming in 1869.

In 1869 the two railroads met at Promontory, Utah. Huge parades and celebrations took place as the final spike was hammered into place. The railroad would change Wyoming forever.

BECOMING A TERRITORY

When track crews came through Wyoming to lay rails, towns sprang up along the railroad route. Laborers needed places to eat, sleep, and have fun. Some businesspeople thought feeding and housing these workers would be a good opportunity to make money. In May 1867, they started building a town called Cheyenne, after the Cheyenne Indians. By August, Cheyenne had formed a temporary government and elected its first mayor. By the time the railroad got there five months later, its population had grown to 4,000, making it the largest city in the Dakota Territory. Other towns also grew up along the path of the railroad, such as Laramie, Rawlins, Rock Springs, and Evanston.

As the population grew, the people clamored for a territory of their own. At that time, Wyoming did not have the boundaries it does today. Before it became

The railroad helped to create successful and busy towns such as Cheyenne.

Wyoming, this land was divided among the Dakota, Utah, and Idaho territories.

It was not until the late 1860s—and the coming of the railroad—that borders were drawn and a name was chosen for the brand-new Wyoming Territory. *Wyoming* is an Algonquin Indian word meaning "large prairie place." In 1868, Wyoming became a territory. Just two years later, Wyoming's population was 9,118.

ATTRACTING SETTLERS

To attract more settlers to new western territories, the United States government passed the Homestead Act. This act gave people free land if they promised to farm it for a specific amount of time, usually five years. The first homesteaders came to Wyoming in the 1870s.

The new territory's government also wanted to draw more women to the territory, because a larger population would help support Wyoming's claims to becoming a state someday. Because there were so few comforts of civilization and so few job opportunities for women, few came to settle there who were not already married. As a result, Wyoming's many single men had a hard time finding brides. Without the opportunity to marry and raise a family, these men would most likely leave Wyoming at some point.

Hoping to make the territory more attractive for women, a legislator named William Bright introduced a bill (proposed law) in Wyoming's territorial congress that would allow women to vote. In 1869 the law passed, and history was made—Wyoming Territory was the first to allow women the right to vote. One European king sent a telegram to congratulate Wyoming for this practice of "progress, enlightenment, and civil rights in America." It would be another half century before a similar law was passed in the United States Congress.

The women of Wyoming were also the first in the nation to hold public office. Esther Hobart Morris became the first woman ever to take on the job of justice of the peace. (Justices of the peace are responsible for hearing court cases involving minor crimes, such as shoplifting.) Wyoming women were also the first to serve on juries. A jury is a group of citizens who hear evidence in a court of law and make decisions based on the facts. The idea of women serving on juries was considered so unusual that newspapers from the East sent reporters to cover trials in Wyoming. But the women's right to sit on juries did not last long. Some men considered the practice unladylike and fought against it. In 1871 the practice of using women on juries was stopped and did not resume until 1950.

In 1870, women waited in line to vote for the first time.

The government's plan to attract new settlers had worked, but it was not enough. In 1888 the Wyoming territorial government sent the United States Congress a petition asking that Wyoming be admitted to the Union as a state. The first bill did not pass, because Wyoming had a population of only 62,555. The following year, 49 men gathered in Cheyenne to write Wyoming's constitution, a document containing laws and principles by which the state would be governed. It was quickly passed by Wyoming's voters.

Congress approved statehood in 1890. On July 10, President Benjamin Harrison signed a bill making Wyoming the forty-fourth state. Its capital was Cheyenne, chosen because it was the state's largest and most important city. Wyoming's first governor was Francis E. Warren.

FRONTIER DAYS IN THE WILD WEST

Wyoming's population continued to increase in the years after statehood. By 1900 the population was 92,531. Still, Wyoming was a land where there was hardly a person "as far as the eye could see." But to some, it was too crowded.

In those days, Wyoming was truly the Wild West, a frontier where all kinds of things could happen. Rough, raw towns grew overnight. The railroads lured all kinds of people west with advertisements about the healthful climate and wonderful life there. Some were farmers and ranchers, some were miners, and some set up shop in small towns.

(opposite)
Gambling was a common pastime at Cheyenne's many saloons.

While many settlers were honest and hard-working, some people came west to get rich and were not particular about how they got that way. Wyoming's land and resources were up for grabs. Rich people grabbed huge amounts of land. Others scrambled for gold and anything else they could get.

Many famous outlaws, including Butch Cassidy, hid at the Hole in the Wall in north-central Wyoming. Located in the middle fork of the Powder River Canyon, in Johnson County, it is a wall that juts out into a 1,000-foot- (305-m-) deep canyon. The wall has a "hole," or natural cavern, in it.

WHO'S WHO IN WYOMING?

Butch Cassidy (1866–1909), born Robert Parker, was given his name by a fellow outlaw because he worked in a butcher shop. Cassidy robbed trains. He went to jail in 1894 but was offered a pardon by Wyoming's governor if he promised to "leave Wyoming alone." Instead, he and another crook, named Harry Long-baugh (the Sundance Kid), organized a gang called the Wild Bunch. Together they committed many train robberies, always avoiding police capture. Later they escaped to South America and disappeared.

On the long journey from Texas to Wyoming, cowboys braved treacherous rivers and unpredictable weather.

People were not the only ones crowding the state. Cattle were also plentiful in Wyoming. In 1865, some smart businessmen hired cowboys to drive herds of cattle all the way north from Texas. Texas had huge numbers of cattle that had their origin in tiny herds brought by the Spanish in the 1700s. These cattle thrived on Wyoming's ranges. Between 1867 and 1890, cowboys drove ten million head of Texas longhorn cattle up to the rich rangeland of Wyoming. They pushed herds of about 2,000 cattle at a time 12 to 15 miles (19 to 24 km) per day. Cowboy life was hard. The early cowboys "had no tents," one cowboy recalled, "[and] cornmeal and bacon for grubs."

For the cattle owners, however, life was easy. Cowboys worked for low wages, and the owners kept their cows on the open rangeland for free. It also did not cost anything to feed the cattle, because they ate the grass that was already there. Once a year, the owners rounded the cattle up, sent them East on the trains, and sold them for lots of money.

Cattle owners soon became rich. In 1873 ranchers formed what would become the Wyoming Stock Growers' Association (WSGA). By 1885 the WSGA's 400 members owned two million head of cattle and were worth $100 million. Not all of these owners came from Wyoming. Some cattle investors were from the East, or even from England, and had let managers oversee their herds. The cattle barons' money bought them a lot of influence with legislators (lawmakers). In fact, some of them became Wyoming's state leaders.

In 1884 a law was passed saying that mavericks—unbranded cattle—living on the range could not be taken by just anyone. (Cattle owners burn a brand, or symbol of ownership, into cattle's hides as proof of ownership.) It would be easy for a cattle thief to round up these unbranded calves and claim them as their property. That is why the law against claiming unbranded mavericks was passed.

Soon there were so many cattle in Wyoming that the plains became overcrowded. Then came the winter of 1886–1887. It started with an October storm, when snow fell one inch per hour for sixteen hours straight. Next came weeks of record cold, with temperatures plummeting to –46° F (–43° C). A 72-hour-long blizzard followed. By the time spring came, huge herds of cattle were dead. Many cattle companies lost between three and nine of every ten cattle they owned. The air stank as thousands of dead cattle rotted in the fields. Ranchers called it The

Raising cattle was big business in Wyoming.

Great Die-Up. After that, ranching continued in Wyoming on a much smaller scale.

During this time, another type of herd had also been established in Wyoming. A few shepherds brought their sheep to Fort Bridger in 1845. More came in 1869. The sheep thrived in Wyoming's dry areas and cold weather. By 1886 the sheep population had increased to more than 500,000. In 1906 there were more than 4,300,000 of the woolly creatures in Wyoming.

There were many conflicts among sheep ranchers, cattle ranchers, and farmers. Sheep dirtied the water holes and ate grass so close to the ground that cattle could not reach it. Farmers fenced off their land, angering both cattle and sheep ranchers. Some cattle ranchers also suspected the farmers of being rustlers, or cattle thieves. To discourage shepherding, cattle owners killed sheep, burned shepherds' wagons, and even killed the shepherds. They also took revenge on farmers they suspected of stealing.

The owners of large cattle herds were also suspicious of small cattle herd owners. They believed that the owners of smaller ranches were stealing mavericks for themselves. In 1892, hoping to drive small ranchers out of Johnson County, the WSGA hired gunmen from Texas to scare them away. The Invaders, as they were called, shot two rustlers, but the rustlers fought back, and the Invaders slipped away. They were

stopped by federal troops before they could kill again. This event was called the Johnson County War.

Later that year, Wyoming cattlemen hired a gunman named Tom Horn to police the area. Horn shot at farmers, squatters, and rustlers. He put a rock under the head of each of his victims to mark his kills and then charged the cattlemen $600 for each person he killed. This scared away many people. In 1901, he was accused of killing a 14-year-old boy who was tending his sheep. People were furious. Horn was put on trial and executed on November 20, 1903. Some historians now say he was innocent.

The Invaders, who killed two suspected rustlers, were never tried for their crimes.

WATER

While the cattlemen were arguing, Wyoming's farmers were struggling with their own problems. Wyoming was not always a good place to farm. Mapmakers called the Great Plains—especially the drier western parts—the Great American Desert because it was arid (dry) and therefore difficult to farm.

If Wyoming farmers wanted to grow crops, they needed a way to make sure the crops could be watered regularly. John Wesley Powell, a geographer and explorer, reported that Wyoming would not develop unless huge dams and canals were built so that land could be irrigated. Irrigation is a system for watering land through pipes or ditches. The government agreed. At around the turn of the twentieth century, large irrigation projects were undertaken, and farming became more practicable. Now some parts of the plains support huge farms.

WYOMING IN THE TWENTIETH CENTURY

The population grew quickly until 1910, when growth slowed. In 1917, Wyoming sent 11,393 soldiers to fight in World War I (1914–1918), a war with Germany and its allies on one side and Great Britain, France, the United States, and their allies on the other.

In the 1920s a Wyoming landmark became famous for one of the greatest political scandals in United States history. In 1922, Albert Fall, the U.S. Secretary of the Interior, secretly leased a government-owned oil field in Wyoming to two oil companies. The companies took millions of barrels of oil out of the field, which was called Teapot Dome. Fall got $400,000 in bribes. However, a government investigation uncovered the secret deal. Albert Fall went to jail, and Teapot Dome was returned to the government.

In 1929, the Great Depression hit the United States. It was a time of financial hardship for many Americans, including those in Wyoming. The depression happened for a number of reasons. In the 1920s, many people had invested in businesses by purchasing stocks, or shares of various companies. In 1929 the stock market "crashed," and the value of stocks dropped dramatically. Too many people tried to sell their stocks, but no one wanted to buy them, so prices dropped even more.

The famous Teapot Dome scandal inspired cartoons such as this one.

As a result, many people lost money. They could no longer afford to buy things, and many businesses had to close because they could not sell their products. People who worked for those businesses lost their jobs. Many people around the country also lost their homes because they could no longer afford to pay for them. Wyoming was hurt by the depression in many ways, but the state did experience an increase in tourism during the 1930s. Many visitors came to Wyoming "dude ranches." These were places where people could get a taste of cowboy life. Visitors also came to see Yellowstone and other places.

Trail riders enjoy a stay at a Wyoming dude ranch.

The Great Depression gradually came to an end with the start of World War II (1939–1945). The war began in Europe, and at first the United States remained neutral, refusing to take sides. However, in 1941 Japanese fighter planes attacked a United States naval base in Pearl Harbor, Hawaii, and the United States was forced to enter the war. It joined Great Britain, France, and other European countries in fighting against Germany, Italy, and Japan. About 30,000 Wyoming men and women joined the armed services. Wyoming also provided beef, valuable minerals, and other products to help the war effort.

Because of the attack on Pearl Harbor, many people in the United States felt that Japanese-Americans were a threat to the country. Although there was no evidence of this, President Franklin Roosevelt signed an order in 1942 that forced 100,000 Japanese and Japanese-Americans from their homes and into war relocation camps, where they were held prisoner. One of the camps, Heart Mountain Relocation Center, was located between Cody and Powell in Wyoming. At its peak, more than 10,000 Japanese-Americans were imprisoned there.

CHALLENGES FOR THE FUTURE

In the 1970s, mining for coal and drilling for oil and gas became the most important industries in Wyoming, replacing ranching. These industries developed in the regions where the resources were found, especially Wyoming's mineral-rich basins. The state's population nearly doubled because so many people moved there to take mining jobs. In

Coal mines, such as this one near Gillette, are profitable, but can be destructive to the environment.

the 1980s, though, the oil industry became less profitable. Since that time, Wyoming and its economy have been growing very slowly. Many environmentalists fear that as mining extracts oil, gas, uranium, trona, and other resources from the land, some of Wyoming's wild beauty will be destroyed and animals will be harmed. Some people would like to keep the natural beauty pristine, or unspoiled. However, mining also provides jobs and money to those who live in the state.

Despite its natural beauty, Wyoming has a slow growth rate because it has not attracted new industries. There are fewer high-paying professional jobs, such as those in technology or insurance, than there are in other states. One of Wyoming's challenges is to create good job opportunities.

In the 1990s, Wyoming welcomed back one of its natural treasures to Yellowstone National Park—gray wolves. Gray wolves were once native to Wyoming; however, ranchers and farmers worried that these predators would eat their herds. By the late 1920s, wolves had been hunted out of most of the West. In 1995 the United States Fish and Wildlife Service re-introduced wolves into Yellowstone National Park. Some ranchers outside of the park were afraid that these predators would attack their animals. However, most of the wolves stay within Yellowstone, where they are slowly growing in number.

Wyoming has an exciting future ahead. In September 2000, a statue of Chief Washakie, the peaceable Shoshone leader who was once helpful to settlers on their way west, was placed in the United States Capitol in a special ceremony in Washington, D.C. "He always placed the peace and the welfare of this people above all," said Wyoming representative Barbara Cubin. It is that spirit that has served Wyoming well all these years.

Wolves play an important role in the ecosystem, but won't survive without protection.

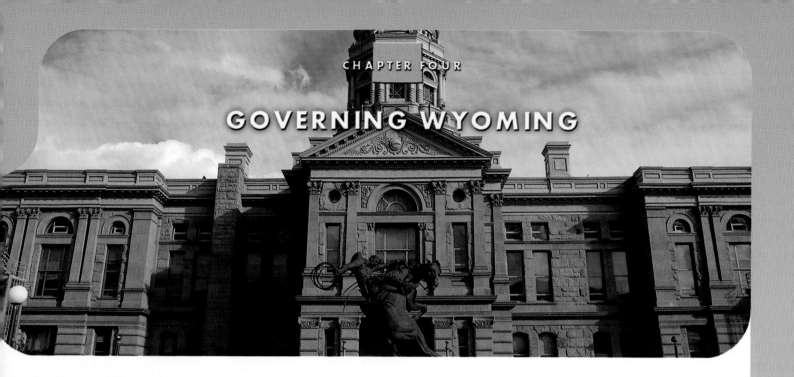

CHAPTER FOUR

GOVERNING WYOMING

The Wyoming state capitol is one of the most important historic buildings in the state.

The Wyoming constitution is a document that defines the laws and principles that govern the state. Wyoming's constitution was created and ratified in 1889. This constitution contained a remarkable provision. "Since equality in the enjoyment of natural and civil rights is only made sure through political equality," the constitution said, "the laws of this state affecting the political rights and privileges of its citizens shall be without distinction of race, color, [or] sex." Wyoming's government was the first in the country to give women the same political rights as men. These rights did not extend to Native Americans at that time.

Wyoming still uses its 1889 constitution. However, lawmakers sometimes make amendments, or changes, to the constitution. The citizens of Wyoming vote on whether to accept or reject an amendment. An amendment becomes law if two-thirds of the legislators (lawmakers) and half of the voters approve it; it must also be signed by the governor. Over the years, dozens of amendments have been added to Wyoming's constitution.

EXECUTIVE BRANCH

The role of the executive branch is to enforce the laws of Wyoming. The governor is head of the executive branch. He or she is elected by the people. The governor's main duty is to see that the state's laws are carried out. Another of the governor's responsibilities is appointing people to run state offices. For example, the governor appoints the attorney general, who represents the state in legal actions such as lawsuits and criminal cases. The governor also selects the heads of state agencies.

Other members of the executive branch include the secretary of state, the auditor, the superintendent of public instruction, and the treasurer. They are all elected to four-year terms, including the governor.

LEGISLATIVE BRANCH

The legislative branch, also called the legislature, passes laws, such as tax, real estate, education, and criminal laws. It also creates a budget, or plan, for spending the state's money. The government collects taxes from state residents to run all the services of the state.

The Wyoming legislature is made up of two parts: the house of representatives and the senate. Wyoming voters elect the members of the

legislative branch. The house has 60 members, called representatives, who serve two-year terms. The senate has 30 members, called senators; each senator is elected for a four-year term. The legislature meets every year. In even-numbered years the legislature holds budget meetings that can last up to 20 days. In odd-numbered years the legislature holds general meetings. These meetings can last up to 40 days.

The House chamber is where representatives gather to discuss new laws.

JUDICIAL BRANCH

The job of the judicial branch is to interpret, or explain, the laws. This is done through the court system, which decides whether someone has broken the law and determines the punishment.

There are different types of courts. Many cases begin in municipal or justice of the peace courts. Municipal courts hear cases involving minor crimes, such as disturbing the peace. Justice of the peace courts can help settle civil cases and resolve small criminal or misdemeanor cases. Many counties also have circuit courts. These courts hear cases involving family violence. They also hear some criminal cases and civil cases involving less than $7,000 in damages.

EXTRA! EXTRA!

Two types of cases go before Wyoming's courts—civil and criminal. Most civil cases involve disputes between two or more parties, in which one or more parties feel that their rights have been violated. A criminal case is one in which a person is charged with committing a crime, such as shoplifting or murder.

WYOMING STATE GOVERNMENT

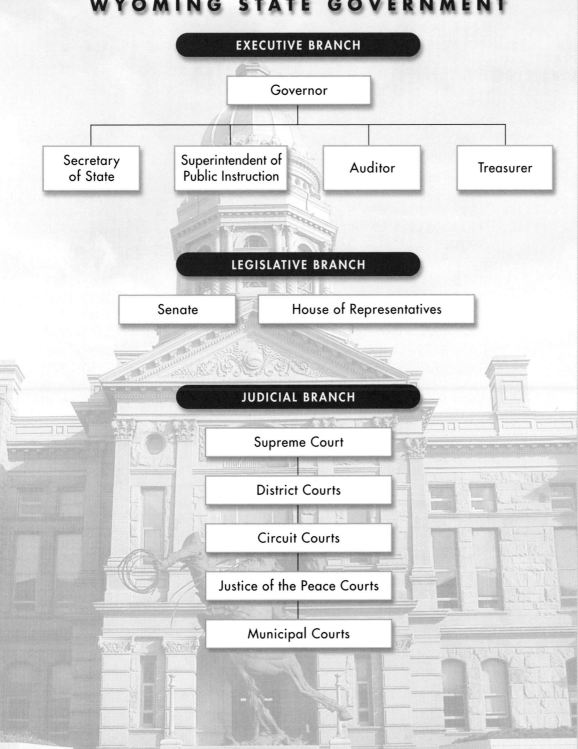

EXECUTIVE BRANCH

Governor

Secretary of State

Superintendent of Public Instruction

Auditor

Treasurer

LEGISLATIVE BRANCH

Senate

House of Representatives

JUDICIAL BRANCH

Supreme Court

District Courts

Circuit Courts

Justice of the Peace Courts

Municipal Courts

WYOMING GOVERNORS

Name	Term	Name	Term
Francis E. Warren	1890	Leslie A. Miller	1933–1939
Amos W. Barber	1890–1893	Nels H. Smith	1939–1943
John E. Osborne	1893–1895	Lester C. Hunt	1943–1949
William A. Richards	1895–1899	Arthur G. Crane	1949–1951
DeForest Richards	1899–1903	Frank A. Barrett	1951–1953
Fenimore Chatterton	1903–1905	C. J. "Doc" Rogers	1953–1955
Bryant B. Brooks	1905–1911	Milward L. Simpson	1955–1959
Joseph M. Carey	1911–1915	J. J. "Joe" Hickey	1959–1961
John B. Kendrick	1915–1917	Jack R. Gage	1961–1963
Frank Houx	1917–1919	Clifford P. Hansen	1963–1967
Robert D. Carey	1919–1923	Stanley K. Hathaway	1967–1975
William B. Ross	1923–1924	Ed Herschler	1975–1987
Frank Lucas	1924–1925	Mike Sullivan	1987–1995
Nellie Tayloe Ross	1925–1927	Jim Geringer	1995–2003
Frank C. Emerson	1927–1931	Dave Freudenthal	2003–
Alonzo M. Clark	1931–1933		

At the next level are district courts. They oversee serious civil and criminal cases. They also hear appeals. An appeal is a request for a higher court to review a case. If a person is not satisfied with a decision made in circuit court, for example, they may request an appeal with the district court.

The highest court in Wyoming is the state supreme court. The supreme court hears appeals from lower courts. The supreme court also decides if a law passed by the legislature is constitutional (in agreement with the constitution) and makes sure that all the courts are working in a fair, efficient manner. It is made up of five justices (judges) who are appointed by the governor. The justices serve eight-year terms but voters may elect them to additional terms.

Cheyenne is the largest city in Wyoming.

TAKE A TOUR OF THE STATE CAPITAL, CHEYENNE

Cheyenne, the capital of Wyoming, is located in the southeastern corner of the state. The town was named for a Native American tribe that once hunted buffalo in the area known as the Great Plains. Cheyenne started as a wild frontier town. It was settled so quickly when the railroad came to town that it was called the Magic City of the Plains.

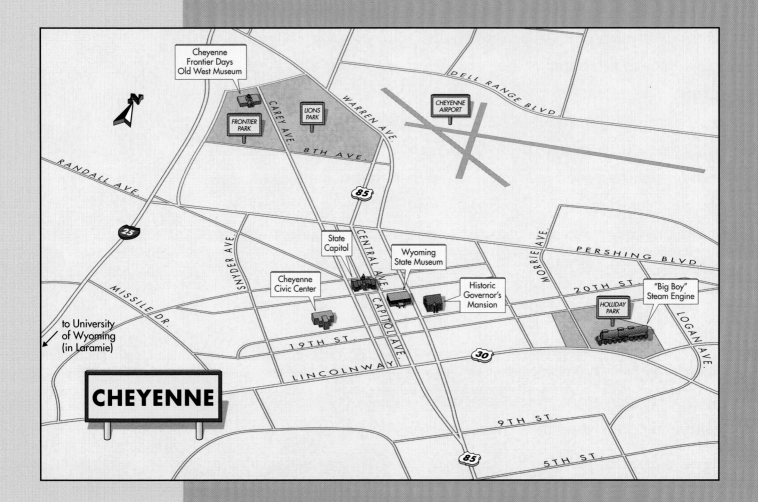

Cheyenne
Frontier Days
Old West Museum

FRONTIER
PARK

CAREY AVE.

LIONS
PARK

8TH AVE.

WARREN AVE.

DELL RANGE BLVD.

CHEYENNE
AIRPORT

RANDALL AVE.

25

85

SNYDER AVE.

State
Capitol

CENTRAL AVE.

CAPITOL AVE.

Wyoming
State Museum

Historic
Governor's
Mansion

MORRIE AVE.

PERSHING BLVD.

20TH ST.

"Big Boy"
Steam Engine

LOGAN AVE.

MISSILE DR.

to University
of Wyoming
(in Laramie)

Cheyenne
Civic Center

19TH ST.

HOLLIDAY
PARK

LINCOLNWAY

30

9TH ST.

85

5TH ST.

CHEYENNE

Cheyenne is home to the state capitol. The capitol cornerstone was laid in May 1887, and the building was completed in 1888. Two additional wings were completed in 1917. The capitol has a 50-foot (15-m) dome covered in gold leaf. The capitol is built of sandstone from Colorado and Rawlins, Wyoming. There are several interesting statues on the capitol grounds. One is *The Spirit of Wyoming,* a statue of a bucking bronco and rider that symbolize the state's cowboy heritage. Another is a statue of Esther Hobart Morris.

Visitors to the statehouse can view the interesting murals (wall paintings) in the senate and house chambers. These colorful paintings depict themes from industry, pioneer life, the law, and transportation. The chambers also have stained-glass ceilings with the state seal in the center.

Just a few blocks from the capitol, you can visit the Wyoming State Museum. A highlight of the museum is the coal exhibit, which shows how important coal mining is to the state. It also has a full-size camptosaurus dinosaur fossil and a hands-on history room for children, which features reproductions of a tepee (a Native American tent) and a chuck wagon (a wagon filled with supplies for a long trail drive), as well as other exhibits. The Historic Governor's Mansion is also nearby. You can take a tour to experience how Wyoming's governors lived from 1905 to 1976. A new governors' residence was built in 1976, in part of Cheyenne's American Legion Park.

Every July, more than 300,000 people attend Cheyenne Frontier Days, the world's largest professional rodeo. The first Cheyenne Frontier Days was held in September 1897. Today, visitors can watch cowboys ride bucking broncos and enjoy parades and Native American dancing. The Cheyenne Frontier Days Old West Museum has a collection of more than 100 old-fashioned horse-drawn carriages.

A bronc rider competes during Cheyenne Frontier Days.

Holliday Park, in downtown Cheyenne, is home to "Big Boy 4004," one of the world's largest steam locomotives. Built to cross the rugged Rocky Mountains, this locomotive could carry 25,000 gallons (94,635 liters) of water at a time, and pull a 3,600-ton (3,658-metric ton) train.

If you go to Old Town Square, prepare to duck. A shoot-out happens almost every day in summer. But don't worry—no one gets hurt, because it is part of a live Wild West show. The cowboy spirit lives on in Cheyenne.

CHAPTER FIVE

THE PEOPLE AND PLACES OF WYOMING

A Shoshone Indian dances on the Wind River Reservation.

Wyoming has the smallest population of any state. With only 493,782 residents as of the year 2000, the population density—the number of people who live within a given area—is very low. There are only about five people per square mile in Wyoming. (The average across the rest of the United States is nearly 80 people per square mile.) Most people are clustered in Wyoming's cities and towns. One-fourth of the population lives in the southeastern cities of Cheyenne, Casper, and Laramie.

Ninety-two in every 100 people in Wyoming are of European ancestry. Many are descended from the pioneers and settlers who came to Wyoming to farm and ranch. Immigrants also came from many places in Europe. For example, many Basque people came from the border of France and Spain to herd sheep. Swedes and Norwegians became loggers. People from Poland came to Sheridan to work as coal miners.

Almost 7 in every 100 people are Hispanic. Many came to Wyoming from Mexico to farm sugar beets and other crops or to work as cowboys. Some of the earliest—and best—cowboys came from Mexico, where they were known as *vaqueros*.

Native Americans make up a little more than 2 in every 100 people. Wyoming is home to the 2-million-acre (809,371-ha) Wind River Reservation. One of the largest reservations in the United States, it is home to about 9,500 eastern Shoshone and northern Arapaho Indians. Every July, sacred dances known as Sun Dances are performed there for three days. There are also powwows and rodeos on the reservation during summer. Powwows are gatherings in which Native Americans connect with each other and their culture by performing sacred dances in traditional dress, singing traditional songs, and preparing and eating traditional foods. They are usually three-day events, and members of other Native American tribes as well as non-Native Americans are invited to attend.

Women have had a big impact on the state. They were pioneers, homesteaders, and schoolteachers. Women also made great strides in politics. America's first woman governor, Nellie Tayloe Ross, was from Wyoming.

WORKING IN WYOMING

As of 1998, nearly 317,000 people in Wyoming worked in jobs other than farming. The mining industry employs almost 18,000 people. Wyoming is ranked sixth in crude oil production. It is also a major source of natural-gas reserves and produces more coal than any other state. Wyoming has the third largest coal reserves in the nation.

Oil refineries, such as Frontier Oil in Cheyenne, process oil for sale in the Rocky Mountain region.

Wyoming mines other minerals as well. It is the leading producer of bentonite, a natural clay used in making a variety of products, from ice cream to kitty litter. The state also has the world's largest supply of trona, or soda ash. It is used in the making of many products, from baking soda to soap. Wyoming also has the nation's second largest supply of uranium, used to produce electricity. Although there are other industries that employ more workers, no industry provides as much money to Wyoming as mining. Minerals contribute about $3.5 billion to the state's economy each year.

About 13,500 people work in manufacturing. Wyoming factories produce clothing and products made from coal. There are also printing and publishing companies. Much manufacturing is done where the necessary raw materials are found. For example, there are sugar beet-processing factories in northeastern Wyoming, where sugar beets are farmed.

Approximately 79,000 workers are employed in the service industry, which includes jobs such as hotel workers and auto mechanics. Many service jobs are related to tourism, the business of providing hotels, entertainment, restaurants, and souvenirs for people who visit the state. More than seven million tourists come to Wyoming each year. Many movies and TV shows have been filmed there, including *Close Encounters of the Third Kind, Rocky IV,* and *The Young Indiana Jones Chronicles.*

A tourist enjoys the scenic beauty of Spring Creek Resort in Jackson Hole.

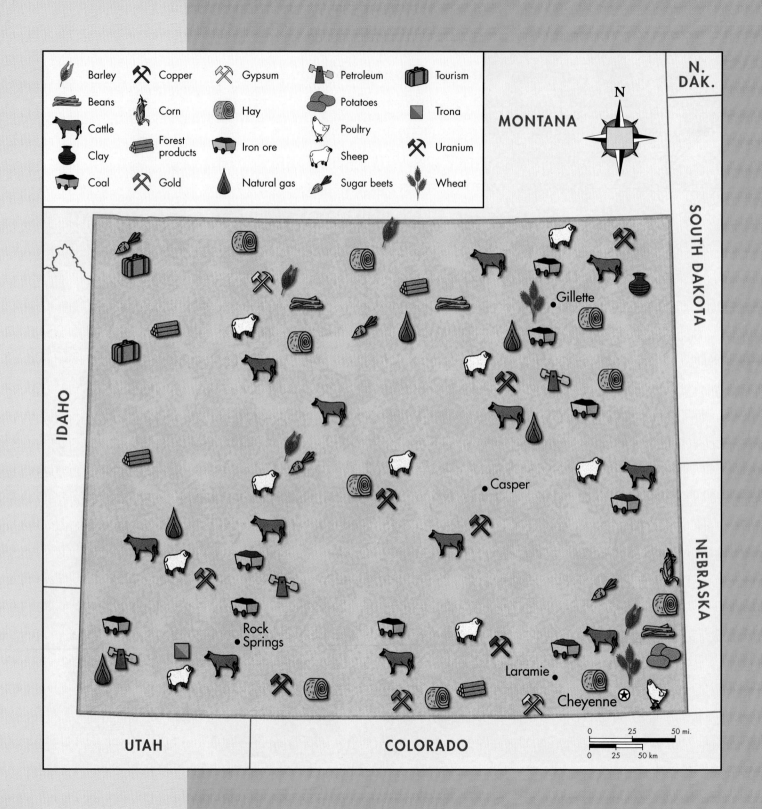

Barley
Beans
Cattle
Clay
Coal
Copper
Corn
Forest products
Gold
Gypsum
Hay
Iron ore
Natural gas
Petroleum
Potatoes
Poultry
Sheep
Sugar beets
Tourism
Trona
Uranium
Wheat

N

MONTANA

N. DAK.

SOUTH DAKOTA

IDAHO

NEBRASKA

UTAH

COLORADO

Gillette

Casper

Rock Springs

Laramie

Cheyenne

0   25   50 mi.

0   25   50 km

Many buffalo call Wyoming home. These big, shaggy beasts have lived on Wyoming's plains for thousands of years. Today, buffalo meat can be found in many supermarkets across the United States. Some companies also sell this tasty meat through the mail. Try the recipe below for an easy way to enjoy buffalo meat. Don't forget to ask an adult for help!

LEMON PEPPER BUFFALO STEAK

buffalo steak medallions
1 lemon
pepper, to taste
3 tablespoons butter

1. Squeeze a lemon onto buffalo steak medallions. Grind pepper on top, and marinate for at least 1 hour.
2. Add butter to a frying pan at medium heat.
3. Panfry medallions at medium heat for four minutes on each side or until they are slightly pink in the middle and brown on the outside, and serve.

Wyoming's 9,200 farms add another $1.5 billion to the state's economy. Beef is still Wyoming's top agricultural product; the state has 1.5 million head of cattle. Wyoming also harvests about $65 million worth of timber from its forests each year.

TAKE A TOUR OF WYOMING

Southeast

More than 11,000 students attend the University of Wyoming.

Southeastern Wyoming is the most populated part of the state. It is the home of Wyoming's capital, Cheyenne, which is the state's largest city. It has a population of about 53,011. From Cheyenne, go west on Route 80 or take the beautiful Happy Jack State Road to Laramie. On the way, you'll see the gigantic Abraham Lincoln Memorial Monument, a 42-foot (13-m) bronze head of our sixteenth president, set on a hill high above the highway.

Laramie is home to the University of Wyoming, the state's only university. One of Laramie's attractions is the Wyoming Territorial Park. At the park you can visit the Wyoming Territorial Prison, where Butch Cassidy was once an inmate before it closed in 1903. The park also contains Frontier Town, where people dressed in old-fashioned costumes reenact the daily lives of early pioneers. If you visit there you can pan for gold or even take a ride in a stagecoach.

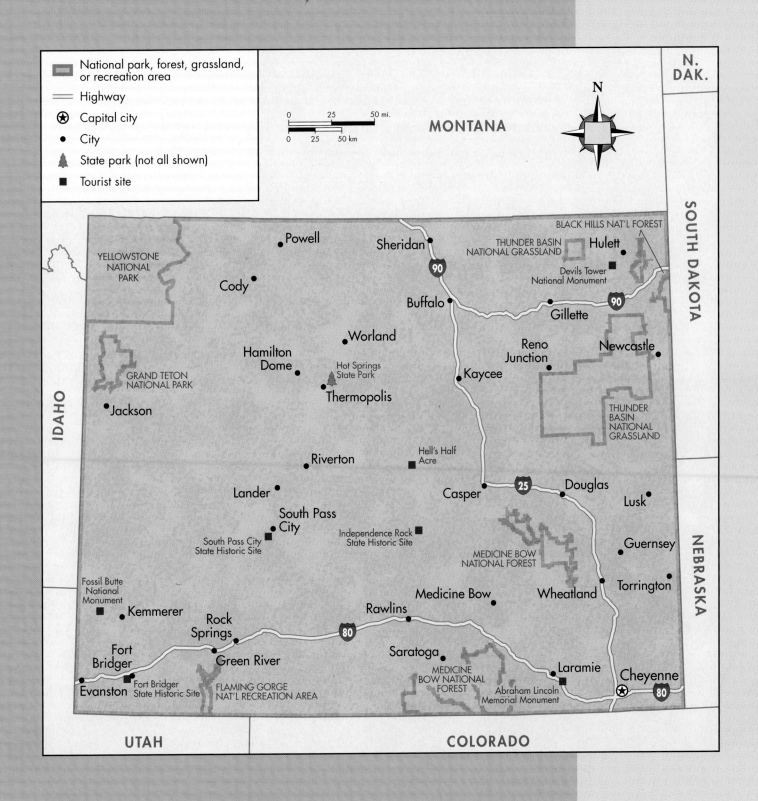

Legend:
- National park, forest, grassland, or recreation area
- Highway
- ⊛ Capital city
- • City
- ▲ State park (not all shown)
- ■ Tourist site

N

0 25 50 mi.

0 25 50 km

MONTANA

N. DAK.

SOUTH DAKOTA

BLACK HILLS NAT'L FOREST

THUNDER BASIN NATIONAL GRASSLAND

• Powell

• Sheridan

Hulett

Devils Tower National Monument ■

90

90

YELLOWSTONE NATIONAL PARK

Buffalo •

• Gillette

• Cody

Worland •

Reno Junction •

Newcastle •

Hamilton Dome •

Hot Springs State Park ▲

Kaycee •

GRAND TETON NATIONAL PARK

Thermopolis

THUNDER BASIN NATIONAL GRASSLAND

IDAHO

• Jackson

Riverton •

Hell's Half Acre ■

Lander •

Casper •

25

Douglas •

Lusk •

South Pass City •

South Pass City State Historic Site

Independence Rock State Historic Site ■

Guernsey •

MEDICINE BOW NATIONAL FOREST

Torrington •

Fossil Butte National Monument ■

• Kemmerer

Medicine Bow •

Wheatland •

NEBRASKA

Rock Springs •

Rawlins •

80

Fort Bridger •

Green River •

Saratoga •

Evanston •

Fort Bridger State Historic Site

FLAMING GORGE NAT'L RECREATION AREA

MEDICINE BOW NATIONAL FOREST

Laramie ■

Cheyenne ⊛

80

Abraham Lincoln Memorial Monument ■

UTAH

COLORADO

Saratoga is a resort town on the other side of the Medicine Bow Mountains. The town boasts a hot-springs swimming pool. The Saratoga National Fish Hatchery is also located there. Trout raised at the hatchery stock lakes and rivers all over the country. You can visit the hatchery to see how fish are farmed.

See history at Independence Rock, a cliff north of Saratoga. Thousands of pioneers on their way west scratched their names on this cliff. Five thousand names and dates are still visible today. Visitors can also see the Oregon Trail Ruts, or grooves in the earth made by wagon wheels. The grooves were created more than 150 years ago, when wagon trains ground across soft sandstone near Guernsey.

Casper is northeast of Independence Rock. Thousands of gallons of oil flow through pipelines in Casper each day. The oil is sent to refineries to be turned into products used for energy throughout the United States, such as heating oil to heat houses and gasoline to fuel vehicles. Casper's attractions include Fort Caspar. The site consists of reconstructed pioneer fort buildings and a museum that includes a feathered Shoshone headdress, arrowheads made by Paleo-Indians, and items relating to Lieutenant Caspar Collins, for whom Casper is named.

You can view soldiers' uniforms and equipment at Fort Caspar.

This area's natural wonders include the Laramie and the Medicine Bow mountain ranges. Medicine Bow National Forest is made up of more than 1 million acres (404,686 ha) spread through five southeastern counties.

Northeast

Much of northeast Wyoming is located on the vast Great Plains, but the far east region is connected to the Black Hills. Though most of these mountains are in South Dakota, 175,000 acres (70,820 ha) of the Black Hills National Forest are in Wyoming. As viewed from the plains, the hills look black because of the thick forests of ponderosa pines that cover them.

To the west the plains are broken up by the Big Horn Mountains. One of the most famous landmarks in this area is Devils Tower National Monument, a gigantic rock column that rises more than

A group of horseback riders pass by Devils Tower National Monument.

FIND OUT MORE

In the Native American legend of Devils Tower, the girls become part of the seven stars of the Pleiades, part of the constellation (a cluster of stars) called Taurus the Bull. Can you find this constellation on a sky chart or in the sky?

1,267 feet (386 m) from the ground. It was formed from the core of an ancient volcano. The grooves in its sides make it look as if the rock has been scratched by a giant bear. In fact, according to an ancient Native American legend, that's just what happened. The story says that young Native American maidens were saved from a bear when they jumped onto a rock and prayed to the Great Spirit. The rock rose up higher and higher. The bear scratched the rock's sides, but the rock kept growing. Finally it rose so high that the girls were pushed into the sky.

The major town in this region is Sheridan. All-American Indian Days are celebrated there, with Native American representatives from all over the country attending. Southwest of Sheridan is the Bradford Brinton Memorial Ranch, which includes 600 pieces of western art.

This region is also home to the Thunder Basin National Grassland, where buffalo once roamed. Hell's Half Acre lies northwest of Casper. A strange landscape of caverns, crevices, and rock towers covers this 320-acre (129-ha) area.

Southwest

Fewer people live in all of southwestern Wyoming than in greater Cheyenne. This area contains the Great Divide Basin, a wide valley ringed with mountains. Rawlins lies on the eastern side of the basin. It is home to the Old Frontier Prison, which closed in 1981. You can take

Visitors can take a guided tour of the Old Frontier Prison, where more than 1,000 men and 12 women were imprisoned in the late 1800s.

a tour there and still see messages on the walls left by inmates. A famous outlaw named Big Nose George Parrot was hanged in Rawlins. Now it is a center for cattle and sheep ranching.

Traveling northwest, you will reach South Pass City. In the 1820s, this mountain pass was used by fur trappers. In 1867 gold was discovered there, resulting in a sudden gold rush as prospectors tried to find their fortunes. By 1870, South Pass City had a population of 4,000. However, its population shrank over time as the supply of gold was depleted. Now it is a state historic site.

Southwest of South Pass City is the small city of Green River. Two-thirds of the world's commercial supply of trona, or calcium carbonate, comes from the dried lake bed of Lake Goshuite near the town. Five factories in Green River process trona.

A young man poses in a period soldier's uniform at Fort Bridger State Historic Site.

You can see huge cliffs rising 1,500 feet (457 m) above the water at the Flaming Gorge National Recreation Area. Created by a dam on the Green River, Flaming Gorge Lake has 375 miles (604 km) of shoreline. It is popular with many people who like to fish for cutthroat trout. Many beautiful multilayered rock cliffs can be seen there.

The old town of Fort Bridger started out as a fur-trading post in 1842. Soon it became a stop for pioneers on their way west. Still later it served as a supply center for gold prospectors. In 1964 the old fort was restored. At the Fort Bridger State Historic Site visitors can see more than a dozen of the original buildings, including Wyoming's first schoolhouse.

Fossil Butte National Monument is a 1,000-foot (305-m) butte—a cliff with a flat, tablelike top. There are fossils embedded in the butte. Because much of Wyoming was once under water, many of the creatures found there are fossilized ancient fish, such as perch and herring. In

WHO'S WHO IN WYOMING?

James Bridger (1804–1881) was a trapper, guide, and storyteller, as well as an early explorer of Wyoming's Rocky Mountains. Later he built the trading post Fort Bridger, which became an important stop on the Oregon Trail.

fact, Fossil Butte has the world's largest deposit of fossilized fish.

Northwest

Northwestern Wyoming is the most visited part of the state because it is home to Yellowstone National Park. More than 3 million people come to Yellowstone each year. South of Yellowstone is Grand Teton National Park, with more than 2.5 million visitors each year.

Beautiful Grand Teton National Park is home to Wyoming's Grand Teton Peak. The peak, the highest in the Teton Range, rises almost straight up, nearly 1.5 miles (2.4 km) from the bottom of the Jackson Hole Valley. At the base of Jackson Hole is the town of Jackson. This

FIND OUT MORE

Green River is famous for its fossil fish. How were these fossils formed? How old are they?

Jackson Hole attracts skiers with mounds of snow and beautiful scenery.

town was once a hangout for outlaws. Now it is famous as a base for some of the best skiing in the world, in the nearby Tetons.

Near Jackson is the National Elk Refuge. Established in 1912, the refuge covers nearly 25,000 acres (10,117 ha). Every winter, about 9,000 elk graze there. Other creatures also winter in the refuge, including bighorn sheep, moose, and mule deer. During the winter months, visitors can take a special sleigh ride to see the elk.

Hot Springs State Park is located near Thermopolis. It is the site of the world's largest mineral hot springs, known as the Big Springs. More than 3.6 million gallons (13.6 million liters) of boiling-hot water pour out of the Big Springs each day. Minerals dissolved in the water leave behind colorful deposits. You can go swimming in some of the cooled water at a nearby bathhouse.

If you go east from Yellowstone on the Yellowstone Highway, you will come to the town of Cody. It was founded by Buffalo Bill Cody. Cody is another charming "old West" town. Its main attraction is the Buffalo Bill Historical Center, which contains four collections. They are the Plains Indian Museum, the Whitney Gallery of

Western Art, the Cody Firearms Museum, and the Buffalo Bill Museum. Together, they are considered among the finest museums in the West.

There are many more treasures to be found in Wyoming. With its wide-open plains and rugged mountains, the Equality State represents the grandeur of the American West. Welcome to Wyoming!

White patterned tepees stand outside the Buffalo Bill Historical Center in Cody.

WYOMING ALMANAC

Statehood date and number: July 10, 1890/44th state

State seal: Features a woman on a pedestal, holding a banner with the words "Equal Rights." The male figures on either side represent two of the state's leading industries—a cowboy for livestock and a miner for the mining industry. A five-pointed star has the number 44, the number of Wyoming's admission into the Union. The seal also features the dates 1869, when the territorial government was formed; and 1890, the year of statehood. Adopted by the second legislature in 1893, revised in 1921.

State flag: Features the great seal "branded" on a bison. A red border represents Native Americans and the blood of the early pioneers who gave their lives to reclaim the soil. A thin white border represents purity, and blue, the color of the sky and mountains, is symbolic of fidelity and justice. Adopted January 31, 1917.

Geographic center: Fremont, 58 miles (93 km) E-NE of Lander

Total area/rank: 97,914 square miles (253,597 sq km)/9th

Borders: Montana, South Dakota, Nebraska, Colorado, Utah, and Idaho

Latitude and longitude: Wyoming is located approximately between 104° 03' and 111° 03' W and 41° 45' N.

Highest/lowest elevation: Gannett Peak, 13,804 feet (4,207 m) above sea level/Belle Fourche River, 3,099 feet (945 m) above sea level

Hottest/coldest temperature: 114° F (46° C) on July 12, 1900, at Basin/–66° F (–54° C) on February 9, 1933, at Moran

Land area/rank: 97,105 square miles (251,501 sq km)/9th

Total water area/rank: 714 square miles (1,849 sq km)/35th

Population/rank: 493,782 (2000 census)/50th

Population of major cities:

Cheyenne: 53,011

Casper: 49,644

Laramie: 27,204

Origin of state name: Based on an Algonquin Indian word meaning "large prairie place"

State capital: Cheyenne

Counties: 23

State government: 30 senators, 60 representatives

Major rivers/lakes: Platte, Wind, Big Horn, Yellowstone, Snake, Green/Yellowstone, Jackson, Shoshone

Farm products: Wheat, oats, sugar beets, corn, potatoes, barley, alfalfa

Livestock: Sheep, cattle

Manufactured products: Mining products, including refined petroleum; chemical products; lumber and wood products; stone and clay products; wool products; printing and publishing; machinery; sports clothes

Mining products: Oil, natural gas, coal, bentonite, gold, trona, sodium carbonate, uranium

Bird: Western meadowlark

Dinosaur: Triceratops

Fish: Cutthroat trout

Flower: Indian paintbrush

Fossil: Knightia

Mammal: Bison

Motto: "Equal Rights"

Nicknames: The Equality State, Big Wyoming, the Cowboy State

Reptile: Horned toad

Song: "Wyoming"

Stone: Jade

Symbol: Bucking cowboy

Tree: Plains cottonwood

Wildlife: Bears, deer, moose, elk, bighorn sheep, wolves, grouse, pheasants, bass, perch

TIMELINE

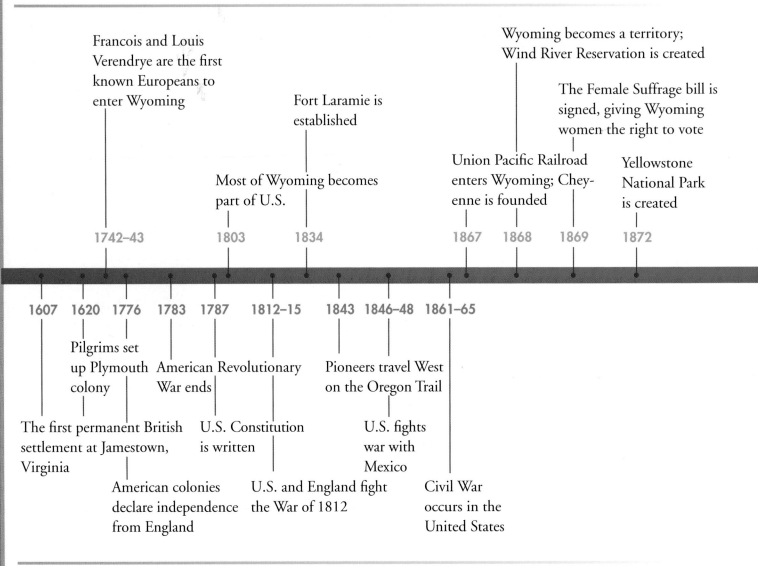

Francois and Louis Verendrye are the first known Europeans to enter Wyoming

Wyoming becomes a territory; Wind River Reservation is created

Fort Laramie is established

The Female Suffrage bill is signed, giving Wyoming women the right to vote

Most of Wyoming becomes part of U.S.

Union Pacific Railroad enters Wyoming; Cheyenne is founded

Yellowstone National Park is created

1742–43   1803   1834   1867   1868   1869   1872

1607   1620   1776   1783   1787   1812–15   1843   1846–48   1861–65

Pilgrims set up Plymouth colony

American Revolutionary War ends

Pioneers travel West on the Oregon Trail

The first permanent British settlement at Jamestown, Virginia

U.S. Constitution is written

U.S. fights war with Mexico

American colonies declare independence from England

U.S. and England fight the War of 1812

Civil War occurs in the United States

UNITED STATES HISTORY

72

First national monu-
ment, Devils Tower,
is created

Nellie Tayloe Ross
becomes first
woman governor
in U.S.

Heart Mountain Relocation
Center established in Park
County

Wolves are reintroduced
to Yellowstone National
Park

Uranium is
discovered in
Lusk

Dick Cheney
is elected vice
president of
the United
States

More than one
million acres
burned in forest
fires at Yellow-
stone National
Park

Wyoming
becomes the
44th state

One of the greatest
scandals in U.S.,
known as Teapot
Dome, occurs

Trona (soda ash) is
discovered in Sweetwater
County

1890 1906 1918 1922–1927 1925 1939 1942 1988 1995 2000

1917–18 1929 1941–45 1950–53 1964 1965–73 1969 1991 1995

U.S. takes part in
World War I

Civil rights laws
passed in the U.S.

U.S. and other nations
fight in Persian Gulf War

U.S. fights in
World War II

U.S. fights in the
Vietnam War

The stock market
crashes and U.S.
enters the Great
Depression

U.S. fights in the
Korean War

U.S. space shuttle
docks with Russian
space station

Neil Armstrong
and Edwin
Aldrin land on
the moon

GALLERY OF FAMOUS WYOMING PEOPLE

Benjamin de Bonneville

(1796–1878)

Explorer who led an expedition of 110 men to Wyoming. He found oil in the Wind River Basin.

Dick Cheney

(1941–)

Politician. In 2000, he was elected vice president of the United States under George W. Bush. Previously he served as a United States congressman representing Wyoming, and as secretary of defense under President George H. W. Bush. Grew up in Casper.

John Charles Frémont

(1813–1890)

Soldier, explorer, and politician who helped to survey Wyoming and much of the territory west of the Missouri River.

Curt Gowdy

(1919–)

Famous sportscaster, born in Green River. A state park is named after him.

Patricia McLachlan

(1938–)

Award-winning children's-book author. She won the Newbery Award for her sensitive book about frontier life, *Sarah, Plain and Tall.* Born in Cheyenne.

Bill Nye

(1850–1896)

Humorist and newspaper editor. Born in Shirley Mills, Maine; he moved to Wyoming in 1876. He was founder of the Laramie newspaper, *Boomerang,* and wrote humorous stories about frontier life. Nationally famous as a humor writer.

Mary O'Hara

(1885–1980)

Movie screenwriter and author of a number of very popular children's books about horses. Her most famous book was *My Friend Flicka.* Grew up on a ranch near Laramie.

Jackson Pollock

(1912–1956)

Internationally famous artist known for his abstract style of painting, covering canvases with drips of paint. Born in Cody.

Alan K. Simpson

(1931–)

United States senator from Wyoming. He served for 18 years. Born in Cody.

GLOSSARY

amendment: a revision or change

arid: dry

bentonite: a special kind of clay that is used for sealing things

butte: a mountain with steep, clifflike sides and a flat, tablelike top

constitution: a document that outlines the set of laws and/or principles of government

continental divide: an imaginary line separating the continent; on one side of it the rivers flow east; on the other, the rivers flow west

geyser: a hot spring that spurts out steam and water

Hispanic: someone from a Spanish-speaking country or of Spanish descent

hot spring: a natural source of hot water

intermontane: land between mountains

irrigation: supplying land with water through pipes, canals, or ditches

jury: a group of citizens who gather to hear evidence presented in a court of law and make a judgment based on the facts

manufacturing: to make products in large numbers

outlaw: a person who has broken the law and tries to avoid capture

plain: a large, flat piece of land that has few trees

politics: relating to the government

population: the number of people living in a certain area

ratified: confirmed or approved

reservation: a tract of land that has been set aside by the government for use by Native Americans

reservoir: a man-made lake where water is stored for use in irrigation, producing electric power, etc.

rustlers: cattle thieves

scandal: a wrongdoing that becomes widely known

suffrage: the right to vote

telegraph: a device for sending messages over a wire by using a code

tourism: the business of providing food, shelter, and entertainment for visitors

treaty: a formal agreement

trona: the mineral calcium carbonate

uranium: a radioactive material, mined in Wyoming, used to produce energy

FOR MORE INFORMATION

Web sites

Wyoming

http://www.state.wy.us/

Links to information about Wyoming for citizens, businesses, government, and visitors.

State of Wyoming Kid's page

http://www.state.wy.us/kids.asp

Features stories about Wyoming, as well as state symbols and historical facts.

Trib.com

http://www.trib.com/WYOMING/

This newspaper site, run by the Casper *Star-Tribune*, has lots of articles and other information about Wyoming.

The Oregon Trail

http://www.isu.edu/~trinmich/Oregontrail.html

Facts, maps, and information about the Oregon Trail.

Books

Alter, Judy. *Exploring and Mapping the American West.* Danbury, CT: Children's Press, 2001.

Dolan, Edward F. *Beyond the Frontier: The Story of the Trails West.* Tarrytown, NY: Benchmark Books, 2000.

Robbins, Ken. *Thunder on the Plains: The Story of the American Buffalo.* New York, NY: Atheneum, 2001.

Swinburne, Stephen R. *Once a Wolf: How Wildlife Biologists Fought to Bring Back the Gray Wolf.* New York, NY: Houghton Mifflin Co., 1999.

Addresses

Wyoming Tourism

Interstate-25 at College Drive
Cheyenne, WY 82002

Governor's Office

State Capitol, Room 124
Cheyenne, WY 82002

INDEX

79

MEET THE AUTHOR

When **Alexandra Hanson-Harding** was a teenager, her parents stuffed her and her little brothers and sisters into a station wagon and took them on a camping trip across the country. One of the most unforgettable places she saw was Wyoming, from the majestic Tetons to the bubbling mud flats of Yellowstone National Park. To write this book, Alexandra made phone calls, read books, and did lots of web surfing, in addition to recalling good memories. And of course she shared the buffalo she cooked with her husband, Brian, and sons, Moses, 12, and Jacob, 9.

Photographs © 2003: AP/Wide World Photos/E N Smith: 42; Archive Photos/Getty Images: 18 (Kean), 68; Bridgeman Art Library International Ltd., London/New York: 23 bottom (Private Collection, Ken Welsh); Brown Brothers: 55, 66 bottom; Corbis Images: 33 left, 39 (Bettmann), 33 right (Jonathan Blair), 74 top left (Larry Downing/Reuters NewMedia Inc.), 67 top (Layne Kennedy), 65 (Michael S. Lewis), 69 (Kevin R. Morris), 8 (David Muench), 16, 43 (Jeff Vanuga), 40, 74 top right; Culver Pictures: 23 top; Dembinsky Photo Assoc.: 15 (Willard Clay), 71 bottom left (Alan G. Nelson), 7, 12 top (Scott T. Smith); Getty Images/Barbara Ries: 74 bottom right; H. Armstrong Roberts, Inc.: 62, 66 top (W.J. Scott), 46 (D&P Valenti); ImageState/Michele & Tom Grimm: 67 bottom; Jeff Vanuga: 17 (Ovis), 14, 54; MapQuest.com, Inc.: 70 bottom; Mary Liz Austin: 3 right, 13; Network Aspen/Jeffrey Aaronson: 52; North Wind Picture Archives: 21, 19, 22, 24, 26, 34; Photo Researchers, NY: 71 top right (C.K. Lorenz), 71 bottom right (Rod Planck); Richard L. Gilbert: 44, 47, 71 top left; Stock Montage, Inc.: 28, 31, 74 bottom left; Stone/Getty Images: 12 bottom (Eastcott/Momatiuk), 4 (Suzanne & Nick Geary), 3 left, 9 (Ted Wood); Superstock, Inc.: 70 top; Ted Wood: 57; The Image Works/David Frazier: 63; Tom Dietrich: cover, 56; Tom Till Photography, Inc.: 20; Wind River Photography/Jim Gores: 49, 51, 60; Woodfin Camp & Associates/Don Pitcher: 27; Wyoming State Archives, Division of Cultural Resources: 29, 35, 37.